And know that I am with you always; yes, to the end of time.

Jesus Christ

God never gives someone a gift they are not capable of receiving. If he gives us the gift of Christmas, it is because we all have the ability to understand and receive it.

Pope Francis

Christmas is the perfect time to celebrate the love of God and family and to create memories that will last forever. Jesus is God's perfect, indescribable gift. The amazing thing is that not only are we able to receive this gift, but we are able to share it with others on Christmas and every other day of the year.

Joel Osteen

Maybe Christmas, the Grinch thought, doesn't come from a store.

Dr. Seuss

The spirit of Christmas is the spirit of love and of generosity and of goodness. It illuminates the picture window of the soul, and we look out upon the world's busy life and become more interested in people than in things.

Thomas S. Monson

Expectancy is the atmosphere for miracles.

Edwin Louis Cole

It is a fine seasoning for joy to think of those we love.

Moliere

I stopped believing in Santa Claus when I was six. Mother took me to see him in a department store and he asked for my autograph.

Shirley Temple

Moving between the legs of tables and of chairs, rising or falling, grasping at kisses and toys, advancing boldly, sudden to take alarm, retreating to the corner of arm and knee, eager to be reassured, taking pleasure in the fragrant brilliance of the Christmas tree.

T. S. Eliot

Christmas is the day that holds all time together.

Alexander Smith

The main reason Santa is so jolly is because he knows where all the bad girls live.

George Carlin

Christmas is the spirit of giving without a thought of getting. It is happiness because we see joy in people. It is forgetting self and finding time for others. It is discarding the meaningless and stressing the true values.

Thomas S. Monson

Christmas is not a time nor a season, but a state of mind. To cherish peace and goodwill, to be plenteous in mercy, is to have the real spirit of Christmas.

Calvin Coolidge

Christmas is a season not only of rejoicing but of reflection.

Winston Churchill

The excellence of a gift lies in its appropriateness rather than in its value.

Charles Dudley Warner

Before we took down the tree each year, Dad would always say a prayer that we would be together the next Christmas. I cling to that prayer, which serves as a reminder that it's important to be grateful in the present for the people you love because, well, you never know.

Catherine Hicks

To perceive Christmas through its wrappings becomes more difficult with every year.

E. B. White

There are some people who want to throw their arms round you simply because it is Christmas; there are other people who want to strangle you simply because it is Christmas.

Robert Staughton Lynd

At Christmas our house is like a Donnie and Marie
Christmas Special.

Kevin Richardson

Christmas, my child, is love in action. Every time we love,
every time we give, it's Christmas.

Dale Evans

He who has not Christmas in his heart will never find it
under a tree.

Roy L. Smith

Once again, we come to the Holiday Season, a deeply
religious time that each of us observes, in his own way, by
going to the mall of his choice.

Dave Barry

I once wanted to become an atheist, but I gave up - they
have no holidays.

Henny Youngman

Finding the real joy of Christmas comes not in the hurrying and the scurrying to get more done, nor is it found in the purchasing of gifts. We find real joy when we make the Savior the focus of the season.

Thomas S. Monson

I once bought my kids a set of batteries for Christmas with a note on it saying, toys not included.

Bernard Manning

The two most joyous times of the year are Christmas morning and the end of school.

Alice Cooper

My brothers and sisters, true love is a reflection of the Savior's love. In December of each year we call it the Christmas spirit. You can hear it. You can see it. You can feel it.

Thomas S. Monson

Christmas is doing a little something extra for someone.

Charles M. Schulz

The earth has grown old with its burden of care, but at Christmas it always is young, the heart of the jewel burns lustrous and fair, and its soul full of music breaks the air, when the song of angels is sung.

Phillips Brooks

In our open society, we are inclined to give to the less fortunate for the pure goodness of giving. We open our home to those who are alone on this holiday to spread some warmth into the life of another.

Jeff Miller

'A Christmas Story' has always meant a lot to me personally.

Peter Billingsley

I save every Christmas card. I keep them all.

Alison Sweeney

People say I don't write books, I make Christmas presents.

Bryce Courtenay

Happy, happy Christmas, that can win us back to the delusions of our childhood days, recall to the old man the pleasures of his youth, and transport the traveler back to his own fireside and quiet home!

Charles Dickens

It's true, Christmas can feel like a lot of work, particularly for mothers. But when you look back on all the Christmases in your life, you'll find you've created family traditions and lasting memories. Those memories, good and bad, are really what help to keep a family together over the long haul.

Caroline Kennedy

Every gift which is given, even though is be small, is in reality great, if it is given with affection.

Pindar

God is in the details.

Ludwig Mies van der Rohe

Christmas in Bethlehem. The ancient dream: a cold, clear
night made brilliant by a glorious star, the smell of incense,
shepherds and wise men falling to their knees in adoration
of the sweet baby, the incarnation of perfect love.

Lucinda Franks

Let's be naughty and save Santa the trip.

Gary Allan

Christmas is joy, religious joy, an inner joy of light and
peace.

Pope Francis

If you haven't got any charity in your heart, you have the
worst kind of heart trouble.

Bob Hope

There is no better time than now, this very Christmas
season, for all of us to rededicate ourselves to the principles

taught by Jesus the Christ. It is the time to love the Lord, our God, with all our heart - and our neighbors as ourselves.

Thomas S. Monson

When we were children we were grateful to those who filled our stockings at Christmas time. Why are we not grateful to God for filling our stockings with legs?

Gilbert K. Chesterton

Nothing says holidays, like a cheese log.

Ellen DeGeneres

I will honor Christmas in my heart, and try to keep it all the year.

Charles Dickens

Don't let the past steal your present. This is the message of Christmas: We are never alone.

Taylor Caldwell

What will you and I give for Christmas this year? Let us in our lives give to our Lord and Savior the gift of gratitude by living His teachings and following in His footsteps.

Thomas S. Monson

The supernatural birth of Christ, his miracles, his resurrection and ascension, remain eternal truths, whatever doubts may be cast on their reality as historical facts.

David Friedrich Strauss

Christmas waves a magic wand over this world, and behold, everything is softer and more beautiful.

Norman Vincent Peale

Christmas isn't a season. It's a feeling.

Edna Ferber

The real evidence for Jesus and Christianity is in how Jesus and the Christianity based on him manifest themselves in the lives of practicing Christians.

Lionel Blue

Christmas is a stocking stuffed with sugary goodness.

Mo Rocca

I wrapped my Christmas presents early this year, but I used the wrong paper. See, the paper I used said 'Happy Birthday' on it. I didn't want to waste it so I just wrote 'Jesus' on it.

Demetri Martin

Christmas is a season for kindling the fire for hospitality in the hall, the genial flame of charity in the heart.

Washington Irving

One of the most glorious messes in the world is the mess created in the living room on Christmas day. Don't clean it up too quickly.

Andy Rooney

The Christian faith can never be separated from the soil of sacred events, from the choice made by God, who wanted to speak to us, to become man, to die and rise again, in a particular place and at a particular time.

Pope Benedict XVI

T'was the night before Christmas, when all through the house, not a creature was stirring, not even a mouse.

Clement Clarke Moore

Christmas is a tonic for our souls. It moves us to think of others rather than of ourselves. It directs our thoughts to giving.

B. C. Forbes

As dry leaves that before the wild hurricane fly, when they meet with an obstacle, mount to the sky. So up to the house-top the coursers they flew, with the sleigh full of toys, and St. Nicholas too.

Clement Clarke Moore

Now, the essence, the very spirit of Christmas is that we first make believe a thing is so, and lo, it presently turns out to be so.

Stephen Leacock

I love giving gifts and I love receiving them. I really like giving little kids extravagant gifts. You see their little faces light up and they get excited. If it's a really good gift, I love receiving it, like jewels, small islands.

Gina Gershon

Always be prepared if someone asks you what you want for Christmas. Give brand names, the store that sells the merchandise, and, if possible, exact model numbers so they can't go wrong. Be the type who's impossible to buy for, so they have to get what you want.

John Waters

Christmas is taken very seriously in this household. I believe in Father Christmas, and there's no way I'd do anything to undermine that belief.

Carol Ann Duffy

A good conscience is a continual Christmas.

Benjamin Franklin

The Supreme Court has ruled that they cannot have a nativity scene in Washington, D.C. This wasn't for any religious reasons. They couldn't find three wise men and a virgin.

Jay Leno

Christmas... is not an external event at all, but a piece of one's home that one carries in one's heart.

Freya Stark

What I don't like about office Christmas parties is looking for a job the next day.

Phyllis Diller

We consider Christmas as the encounter, the great encounter, the historical encounter, the decisive encounter, between God and mankind. He who has faith knows this truly; let him rejoice.

Pope Paul VI

Unless we make Christmas an occasion to share our blessings, all the snow in Alaska won't make it 'white'.

Bing Crosby

A lovely thing about Christmas is that it's compulsory, like a thunderstorm, and we all go through it together.

Garrison Keillor

I don't think Christmas is necessarily about things. It's about being good to one another, it's about the Christian ethic, it's about kindness.

Carrie Fisher

Santa Claus has the right idea - visit people only once a year.

Victor Borge

Mail your packages early so the post office can lose them in time for Christmas.

Johnny Carson

At Christmas play and make good cheer, for Christmas comes but once a year.

Thomas Tusser

My brothers and sisters, may the spirit of love which comes at Christmastime fill our homes and our lives and linger there long after the tree is down and the lights are put away for another year.

Thomas S. Monson

Every year we celebrate the holy season of Advent, O God. Every year we pray those beautiful prayers of longing and waiting, and sing those lovely songs of hope and promise.

Karl Rahner

That's the true spirit of Christmas; people being helped by people other than me.

Jerry Seinfeld

I love Christmas, not just because of the presents but because of all the decorations and lights and the warmth of the season.

Ashley Tisdale

At Christmas, 'It's a Wonderful Life' makes me cry in exactly the same places every time, even though I know it's coming.

Nicholas Lea

Christmas is, of course, the time to be home - in heart as well as body.

Garry Moore

I think Christmas is about celebration and come on, on the inside everyone wants to dance.

TobyMac

The thing about Christmas is that it almost doesn't matter what mood you're in or what kind of a year you've had - it's a fresh start.

Kelly Clarkson

Christmas, children, is not a date. It is a state of mind.

Mary Ellen Chase

The sharpest memory of our old-fashioned Christmas eve is my mother's hand making sure I was settled in bed.

Paul Engle

Santa is our culture's only mythic figure truly believed in by a large percentage of the population. It's a fact that most of the true believers are under eight years old, and that's a pity.

Chris Van Allsburg

I'm sure most of us remember being a kid and you have all of this endless time where two weeks before Christmas feels like ten years. I used to go to bed to try and go to sleep to try and make it go faster.

Andrea Arnold

There are a lot of Grinches out there that would like nothing better than to take any references to religion out of the holiday season.

Ernest Istook

I love the excitement, the childlike spirit of innocence and just about everything that goes along with Christmas.

Hillary Scott

Christmas renews our youth by stirring our wonder. The capacity for wonder has been called our most pregnant human faculty, for in it are born our art, our science, our religion.

Ralph W. Sockman

Faith is salted and peppered through everything at Christmas. And I love at least one night by the Christmas tree to sing and feel the quiet holiness of that time that's set apart to celebrate love, friendship, and God's gift of the Christ child.

Amy Grant

I love singing Christmas carols. I know every harmony to every music-hall Christmas song.

Zooey Deschanel

Christmas makes me happy no matter what time of year it comes around.

Bryan White

Pets, like their owners, tend to expand a little over the Christmas period.

Frances Wright

My Christmases have always just been very simple and about family.

Julie Roberts

There's something about a Christmas sweater that will always make me laugh.

Kristen Wiig

Please to put a nickel, please to put a dime. How petitions trickle in at Christmas time!

Phyllis McGinley

Christmas is a time of year that's so romantic.

Katharine McPhee

Coming from Chicago, I like a white Christmas.

Dennis Franz

I get a little behind during Lent, but it comes out even at Christmas.

Frank Butler

During the first 13 centuries after the birth of Jesus in Bethlehem, no one thought of setting up a creche to celebrate Christmas. The pre-eminent Christian holiday was Easter, not Christmas.

Nancy Pearcey

Our children await Christmas presents like politicians getting in election returns: there's the Uncle Fred precinct and the Aunt Ruth district still to come in.

Marcelene Cox

The best Christmas present I got from my husband was a week to do whatever I wanted.

Olivia Williams

Being a traditionalist, I'm a rabid sucker for Christmas. In July, I'm already worried that there are only 146 shopping days left.

John Waters

The upheavals of adolescence silenced 'A Christmas Carol' for a few years. I became a firebrand atheist. Christmas - humbug! Too commercial! Then I became an agnostic. Christmas was a pro-forma affair, basically a chore. Buy mother a book, dad a new tie, my brother and sister small gifts. Pretend thanks for the fountain pens and shirts I received.

Whitley Strieber

As I lay so sick on my bed, from Christmas till March, I was always praying for poor ole master. 'Pears like I didn't do nothing but pray for ole master. 'Oh, Lord, convert ole master;' 'Oh, dear Lord, change dat man's heart, and make him a Christian.'

Harriet Tubman

The truth is the Super Bowl long ago became more than just a football game. It's part of our culture like turkey at Thanksgiving and lights at Christmas, and like those holidays beyond their meaning, a factor in our economy.

Bob Schieffer

I think that 'Ghost Rider: Spirit of Vengeance' was mentally taxing, if only because I had to go to a Christmas party shortly after I had wrapped photography in Romania at two in the morning as the Ghost Rider. The invitation had a Christmas ornament on it with Ghost Rider's face on it as a tree.

Nicolas Cage

I've been giving back since I was a teen, handing out turkeys at Thanksgiving and handing out toys at toys drives for Christmas. It's very important to give back as a youth. It's as simple as helping an old lady across the street or giving up your seat on the bus for someone who is pregnant.

Queen Latifah

Christmas gives us the opportunity to pause and reflect on the important things around us - a time when we can look back on the year that has passed and prepare for the year ahead.

David Cameron

My parents were kind of over protective people. Me and my sister had to play in the backyard all the time. They bought us bikes for Christmas but wouldn't let us ride in the street, we had to ride in the backyard. Another Christmas, my dad got me a basketball hoop and put it in the middle of the lawn! You can't dribble on grass.

Jimmy Fallon

I was nine or 10 years old and my father was sacked on Christmas Day. He was a manager, the results had not been good, he lost a game on December 22 or 23. On Christmas Day, the telephone rang and he was sacked in the middle of our lunch.

Jose Mourinho

I quickly discovered that trying to go play golf while living in Manhattan was about as easy as trying to grab a taxi while standing out in front of Saks Fifth Avenue in the freezing rain on the last shopping day before Christmas.

Dan Jenkins

I know that a Christmas tree farm in Pennsylvania is about the most random place for a country singer to come from, but I had an awesome childhood.

Taylor Swift

I loved raising my kids. I loved the process, the dirt of it, the tears of it, the frustration of it, Christmas, Easter, birthdays, growth charts, pediatrician appointments. I loved all of it.

Jane Elliot

'I am a bad mother.' Every Christmas, this is what I think because the holiday season fills me with such anxiety. I'm sure that other mothers are happily baking cookies, decorating trees, and finding perfect gifts for everyone.

Tess Gerritsen

I beg to present you as a Christmas gift the city of Savannah.

William Tecumseh Sherman

It is never too late to get into tennis! While I started playing at the age of 8 when my parents gave me a tennis racquet for Christmas, tennis is a lifelong sport that can be enjoyed by people of almost any age. It's also something you never forget once you learn.

Samantha Stosur

When I cook for my family on Christmas, I make feijoada, a South American dish of roasted and smoked meats like ham, pork, beef, lamb, and bacon - all served with black beans and rice. It's festive but different.

Maya Angelou

Don't send funny greeting cards on birthdays or at Christmas. Save them for funerals, when their cheery effect is needed.

P. J. O'Rourke

If you want me to sing this Christmas song with the feeling and the meaning, you better see if you can locate that check.

Mahalia Jackson

For many, Christmas is also a time for coming together. But for others, service will come first.

Queen Elizabeth II

Christmas is far and away my favorite holiday. I love everything about it, from the event that inspired it, hoping for a white one, to wrapping presents. But mostly I love having family and friends gathered, and sharing traditions.

Ellen Hopkins

I think that there are a lot of really beautiful Christmas carols, and then sometimes there are horrible renditions of them that are played to death in malls that make me sad. I try to avoid stores where they're playing bad versions of Christmas songs on repeat.

Gillian Jacobs

Several years ago, I was creating a Christmas present for the family, a self-published cookbook featuring recipes my grandmother had collected and created over decades. While interviewing her for the biographical section, she began to talk about her courtship with my late grandfather.

Kristina McMorris

Christmas is a holiday that persecutes the lonely, the frayed, and the rejected.

Jimmy Cannon

Now I'm an old Christmas tree, the roots of which have died. They just come along and while the little needles fall off me replace them with medallions.

Orson Welles

Christmas carols always brought tears to my eyes. I also cry at weddings. I should have cried at a couple of my own.

Ethel Merman

My favorite traditional Christmas movie that I like to watch is All Quiet on the Western Front. It's just not December without that movie in my house.

Tom Hanks

I've always loved Christmas and that's not really gone away from me from being a child to now. It's always a magical time and I'm unashamed in my love for Christmas.

Martin Freeman

Come Christmas Eve, we usually go to my mom and dad's. Everybody brings one gift and then we play that game when we all steal it from each other. Some are really cool, others are useful and some are a bit out there.

Amy Grant

On the whole, I prefer Christmas as an adult than I did as a child.

Nigella Lawson

I stone got crazy when I saw somebody run down them strings with a bottleneck. My eyes lit up like a Christmas tree and I said that I had to learn.

Muddy Waters

Christmas lights may be the loneliest thing for me, especially if you mix them up with reindeers and sleighs. I feel alone. I feel isolated. I feel I do not belong.

Mira Nair

I like to spend Christmas with family and friends, pigging out, exchanging gifts and basically doing nothing.

George Kotsiopoulos

Dad bought me a toy drum one Christmas, and I eventually destroyed it. I wanted a real drum and he bought me a snare drum. Dad continued to buy me one drum after the other.

Keith Thibodeaux

On Christmas morning, before we could open our Christmas presents, we would go to this stranger's home and bring them presents. I remember helping clean the house up and putting up a tree. My father believed that you have a responsibility to look after everyone else.

George Clooney

We are each one on a road going toward home, but we're not trying to get there for Christmas. We're trying to get there for eternity. We want to arrive home safely to our loving Father in Heaven. He wants us to make it safely there, so He has sent a guiding light for us to follow: a Savior, the Lord Jesus Christ, the perfect example.

Margaret D. Nadauld

At the heart of every really good Christmas movie is the threat, I suppose, to Christmas. Something is wrong with Christmas, in all of these movies. In 'The Polar Express,' there's a kid that doesn't really believe, and that's the threat to Christmas. In 'Santa Claus: The Movie,' jealousy and greed are threatening to overrun his Christmas.

James McAvoy

At Christmas, it's my siblings running around the house, we're cooking, talking, laughing, loud and just crazy. It's beautiful chaos.

Tika Sumpter

When you have kids, you instantly feel that you do not want to do them wrong. Those dads that go off to Florida and start a new life, I couldn't imagine that: seeing my kid once every Christmas, every three years. If I'm gone for six days it feels like too much.

Adam Carolla

We try to make the name longer and longer every year. First, it was 'Larry the Cable Guy's Christmas Spectacular.' Then it was 'It's a Very Larry Christmas.' Now it's 'Larry the Cable Guy's Hula-palooza Christmas Luau.' I'll tell you what it is: It's funny. That's what it is. Who cares what the name of it is? It is a funny special.

Larry the Cable Guy

I was born with an extremely negative attitude. I was the kid who wouldn't smile in Christmas photos, was a poor sport, and hated a lot of things. I eventually grew out of my negativity when I matured.

Colton Haynes

I just think that it's strong and it's important that we recognize what the Christmas season is about; it's about the birth of our Savior, and there's a lot of pressure today to be politically correct, but people are realizing, too, that you have to be open to express your faith what you want believe.

Joel Osteen

Having a birthday cake squashed into your face by young kids? Delicious. I always don a Santa suit at Christmas. Remaining childish is a tremendous state of innocence.

John Lydon

Globalization has created this interlocking fragility. At no time in the history of the universe has the cancellation of a Christmas order in New York meant layoffs in China.

Nassim Nicholas Taleb

What I'm not saying is that all government spending is bad. It's not - far, far from it, but there is no free lunch, as a former colleague of mine used to say. There is no public tooth fairy. Father Christmas does not work on the Treasury staff this year. You can never bail someone out of trouble without putting someone else into trouble.

Arthur Laffer

We should declare war on North Vietnam. We could pave the whole country and put parking strips on it, and still be home by Christmas.

Ronald Reagan

I detest 'Jingle Bells,' 'White Christmas,' 'Rudolph the Red Nosed Reindeer,' and the obscene spending bonanza that nowadays seems to occupy not just December, but November and much of October, too.

Richard Dawkins

Our many different cultures notwithstanding, there's something about the holidays that makes the planet communal. Even nations that do not celebrate Christmas can't help but be caught up in the collective spirit of their neighbors, as twinkling lights dot the landscape and carols fill the air. It's an inspiring time of the year.

Marlo Thomas

I have a musical called Goodbye and Good Luck, based on a Grace Paley short story. I also have King Island Christmas, and there are 20 different productions of it this year.

David Friedman

I am a veteran of the War on Christmas. I am just emerging from a battlefield strewn with dead trees and torn shreds of brightly colored wrapping paper.

Henry Rollins

No matter what, I always make it home for Christmas. I love to go to my Tennessee Mountain Home and invite all of my nieces and nephews and their spouses and kids and do what we all like to do - eat, laugh, trade presents and just enjoy each other... and sometimes I even dress up like Santa Claus!

Dolly Parton

Back in 1960 at Christmas time, I did work loading and unloading boxcars for Railway Express. That was a kind of weight training that helped me. I weighed about 160 when I started. I began to gain weight and kept right on gaining until I reached 195 pounds.

Pete Rose

The Earth reminded us of a Christmas tree ornament hanging in the blackness of space. As we got farther and farther away it diminished in size. Finally it shrank to the size of a marble, the most beautiful marble you can imagine.

James Irwin

My fondest memories are generally the day after Thanksgiving. I get the total decorating Christmas itch.

Katharine McPhee

I have a love/hate relationship with Amy Grant, but I do go back to her Christmas albums once in a while. They're dated and sentimental and the production is nearly unlistenable, but there's something about her vocal performance that just feels really true. I would take her Christmas albums over Mariah Carey's or Destiny's Child's any day.

Sufjan Stevens

It is always weird to be in the studio working on Christmas music in June and July, so we decorated the entire studio, we really did. We brought out lights, fake trees and decorated the place to get in the Christmas spirit. You'd leave the studio, and it'd be 100 degrees out in Nashville, but nonetheless, a great experience.

Dave Haywood

It's silly talking about how many years we will have to spend in the jungles of Vietnam when we could pave the whole country and put parking stripes on it and still be home by Christmas.

Ronald Reagan

When you give up yourself, that's when you will feel the true spirit of Christmas. And that's giving that's serving others and that's when you feel fulfilled.

Joel Osteen

Christmas is the time when kids tell Santa what they want and adults pay for it. Deficits are when adults tell government what they want and their kids pay for it.

Richard Lamm

I think we've taken the meaning of Christmas out. People don't stop and think about Jesus or the birth of Jesus. When they think of Christmas, they think of Santa Claus and - for the children, and they think of giving gifts and out-giving the next person of spending their time looking for the right thing for somebody who has everything.

Billy Graham

In the United States Christmas has become the rape of an idea.

Richard Bach

Even though we're a week and a half away from
Thanksgiving, it's beginning to look a lot like Christmas.

Richard Roeper

I wanted an electric train for Christmas but I got the
saxophone instead.

Clarence Clemons

One of my favorite traditions is that my sisters and I, we all
wear the same pajamas. I've even still got some from when
I was 6. Also, I'll always remember cooking together in the
kitchen and that no matter how busy our schedules are, we
are all together for Christmas.

Bailee Madison

Christmas and the holidays are the season of giving. It's a
time when people are more kind and open-hearted.

Gisele Bundchen

'The Christmas Song,' by Nat King Cole, is not only a
masterful performance; to me it just sounds like the
holidays. I've never sung it, because Nat's version is so

perfect. I gotta leave it alone.

Harry Connick, Jr.

At Christmas, I am always struck by how the spirit of togetherness lies also at the heart of the Christmas story. A young mother and a dutiful father with their baby were joined by poor shepherds and visitors from afar. They came with their gifts to worship the Christ child.

Queen Elizabeth II

God seeks to influence humanity. This is at the heart of the Christmas story. It is the story of light coming into the darkness, of a Savior to show us the way, of light overcoming the darkness, of God's work to save the world.

Adam Hamilton

There's never really been a real hood Christmas movie.

Ice Cube

If you pray enough for things, I am proof that they can happen. I feel like a kid on Christmas day now, every day. It's something I have wanted for a long time and I am as happy as anyone to be here. It is great to be back at my first love.

Robbie Fowler

It always depresses me when people moan about how commercial Christmas is. I love everything about it. The tradition of having this great big feast, slap bang in the middle of winter, is an essential thing to look forward to at the end of the year.

Richard E. Grant

I've got some incredible fans actually - so loyal and they make me birthday cards and Christmas cards. I got this package of poems and artwork based around the songs. They've got this thing called 'Floetry' where they all have to put in artwork. They've set up their own competitions and stuff which is kind of amazing.

Florence Welch

I throw a Christmas party at my house. It's not really a Christmas party, because I don't want to call it a Christmas party. But let's just say I put a lot of Christmas trees around the house, so it smells good.

Bill Murray

Brits and Americans have hundreds of different phrases for the same thing. Luckily, it's usually a source of amusement rather than frustration. A flashlight by any other name is still a torch. My personal favourite is 'fairy lights,' which we boringly refer to as 'Christmas lights.'

Sloane Crosley

You don't want your jewelry to make you look fat. A lot of what's out there now does - you just wind up looking like a Christmas tree.

Padma Lakshmi

Christmas is over and Business is Business.

Franklin Pierce Adams

For me, the spirit of Christmas means being happy and giving freely. It's a tradition for all the kids in the family to help mom decorate the tree. Christmas is all about family, eating, drinking and making merry.

Malaika Arora Khan

I do have a family, and I do have friends, and so-called friends, and acquaintances, and many other people I see only around Christmas time. Maybe they could vouch for me. Maybe they could testify to my existence and save a part of me that thinks I'm no better than a bag of potato chips.

Macaulay Culkin

My favorite toy growing up was Polly Pocket. But one gift that I wanted though never received for Christmas was a pair of trampoline moon shoes. You strap them to your feet and they have springs on them, and you can just jump around!

Lucy Hale

Our traditions have been waking up on Christmas morning and feasting on a southern breakfast. I'm from the South. We eat grits and biscuits and gravy and eggs with Ritz crackers and country ham, bacon, you name it.

Leigh-Allyn Baker

I simply believe food is too good to throw away - and Christmas leftovers can be a gastronomic opportunity for the well-skilled kitchen forager. With a little imagination, there are a million ways to use up leftovers rather than bin them.

Tristram Stuart

One thing I hear a lot is, 'Dude, my mom loves your record,' or 'I got it for my dad for Christmas.' I'm essentially doing dad rock. Which is great, because I love Steely Dan, you know? Nothing wrong with dad rock!

Mac DeMarco

I love the atmosphere at the mall - everything about Christmas. I don't think anything specific gets me in the holiday spirit except for the holidays themselves.

Drake Bell

When I was a child, I was living in the housing projects of Philadelphia. I didn't even have a Christmas tree.

Bill Cosby

There's nothing sadder in this world than to awake Christmas morning and not be a child.

Erma Bombeck

I like the idea of putting your Christmas wish list up and letting people share it.

Bill Gates

Ranking among the greatest Christmas movie classics, 'It's a Wonderful Life' tells a beautiful story about the priceless value of relationships.

John C. Maxwell

My mom always makes the whole family pile into the car and drive around to look at the Christmas lights. My brother and I never want to do it, but my mom just loves it!

Debby Ryan

For more than a decade, I led an organization that put on an elaborate Christmas program each December. It was a big production, with over 250 people participating in more than 20 performances. By the end of the season, everyone who participated was exhausted.

John C. Maxwell

Next to a circus there ain't nothing that packs up and tears out faster than the Christmas spirit.

Kin Hubbard

I suppose if you look back to your early childhood you accept everything people tell you, and that includes a heavy dose of irrationality - you're told about tooth fairies and Father Christmas and things.

Richard Dawkins

My mother was a professional sick person; she took a lot of pain pills. There are many people like that. It's just how they are used to getting attention. I always remember she's the daughter of alcoholics who'd leave her alone at Christmas time.

Jim Carrey

You have to remind kids to stay connected to the meaning of Christmas. Sometimes it takes a little bit of effort, but it's so worth it.

Caroline Kennedy

Christmas morning, I'm going to open presents with my kids. I'm going to take pictures of them opening the presents. Then I'm going to come to the Staples Center and get ready to work.

Kobe Bryant

There's a little vanity chair that Charlie gave me the first Christmas we knew each other. I'll not be parting with that, nor our bed - the four-poster - I'll be needing that to die in.

Helen Hayes

Time always seems long to the child who is waiting - for Christmas, for next summer, for becoming a grownup: long also when he surrenders his whole soul to each moment of a happy day.

Dag Hammarskjold

As we give presents at Christmas, we need to recognize that sharing our time and ourselves is such an important part of giving.

Gordon B. Hinckley

My mother-in-law has come round to our house at Christmas seven years running. This year we're having a change. We're going to let her in.

Les Dawson

Christmas makes everything twice as sad.

Douglas Coupland

It's surprising to me how many of my friends send Christmas cards, or holiday cards, including my atheist and secular friends.

Christopher Hitchens

Bloody Christmas, here again, let us raise a loving cup, peace on earth, goodwill to men, and make them do the washing up.

Wendy Cope

No matter what else is going on, Christmas is my all-time favorite period in the year. It has a positive effect on me like very little else does, seasonally, that is.

Rush Limbaugh

Christmas can have a real melancholy aspect, 'cause it packages itself as this idea of perfect family cohesion and love, and you're always going to come up short when you measure your personal life against the idealized personal lives that are constantly thrust in our faces, primarily by TV commercials.

Dan Savage

November is auspicious in so many parts of the country: the rice harvest is already in, the weather starts to cool, and the festive glow which precedes Christmas has began to brighten the landscape.

F. Sionil Jose

I remember a great America where we made everything. There was a time when the only thing you got from Japan was a really bad cheap transistor radio that some aunt gave you for Christmas.

Cher

Giving is a really big thing around Christmas, as well it should be. Christmas is about giving, and it all stems from the greatest gift the world has ever received - the gift of

Jesus Christ.

Monica Johnson

Christmas to a child is the first terrible proof that to travel hopefully is better than to arrive.

Stephen Fry

I would like to go back and spend a Christmas with my family and myself when I was five years old and just see what that dynamic would be like. Observe it. I think it would be a magical gift.

Sharon Lawrence

If you do good work, it tends to stick around. People still come up to me and say, "The Ref' is my favorite Christmas movie.'

Denis Leary

On Christmas, my family and I see a movie and go out for Chinese food. We don't celebrate Christmas in the traditional sense, in that we do not actually celebrate Christmas.

Eden Sher

My mother was a not-too-devoted atheist. She went to Episcopal church on Christmas Eve every year, and that was mostly it.

Anne Lamott

For me growing up, Christmas time was always the most fantastic, exciting time of year, and you'd stay up until three in the morning. You'd hear the parents wrapping in the other room but you knew that also, maybe, they were in collusion with Santa Claus.

Chris Pine

When I was 12, all I wanted for Christmas was a trampoline or a four-wheeler. I ended up getting both presents for Christmas.

Chris Brown

One thing I love about Christmas music is that it has a tradition of warmth.

Zooey Deschanel

Christmas is more stressful with present buying and making sure everyone gets included, but Thanksgiving is really not that. I don't ever really get stressed out about the food.

Sandra Lee

Why not share with the world the way it is and tell them my feelings about my cat, and how I played with my kids, and how addicted to Christmas time I am, and the smell of pine needles and hearing my kids laugh.

Steven Tyler

Online, there's no time. It's always Christmas.

Lewis Black

Pfft, I hate Christmas Day. It's for children and families. Not for people like me.

Karl Lagerfeld

Religious symbols should be visible in public space, in a dignified and non-provocative manner. Christmas trees here, Jewish menorahs there and, further along, a minaret -

these symbols represent human life in all its diversity.

Tariq Ramadan

As a child, I was bonkers for Christmas. The entire month of December, I couldn't sleep at night from anticipation.

Rosecrans Baldwin

The word of God is very important to Christmas. For unto us a child was born, and we should be reminded of how Christ's amazing journey came to be.

Monica Johnson

I remember driving to North Carolina when I was a little girl in a snowstorm to get down to my mom's family in the Carolinas. There were chains on the car - it was the late sixties - and we were just singing in the car. Christmas carols.

Tori Amos

Christmas is a time when kids tell Santa what they want and adults pay for it. Deficits are when adults tell the government what they want - and their kids pay for it.

Richard Lamm

I like indoor Christmas trees. And I like people who decorate their homes with lights and all that crap. I think it's a healthy outlet for them. If they weren't covering their lawns with twinkling lights, they'd be doing something that was really, really creepy.

Lewis Black

Classic Christmas cookies are really time-consuming. Instead, make a bar you can bake in a pan and just cut up, like a brownie or a blondie or a shortbread, which still has that Christmas vibe.

Zooey Deschanel

Christmas is a rare occasion when we are reminded that we have obligations to people we did not choose to be related to, and that love is not just a spontaneous feeling but something we sometimes really have to work at, with people we may not even much like.

Julian Baggini

There is a lot to celebrate about that little Babe who was

laid in a manger. Christians celebrate Christmas because they are thankful for the promise of salvation, which was delivered in human flesh and named Jesus.

Monica Johnson

I'm not going to tell you to meditate on what Christmas really means and be thankful.

Monica Johnson

It doesn't bother me a bit when people say, 'Merry Christmas' to me. I don't think they are slighting me or getting ready to put me in a ghetto. In fact, I kind of like it.

Ben Stein

The truth is that our way of celebrating the Christmas season does spring from myriad cultures and sources, from St. Nicholas to Coca-Cola advertising campaigns.

Richard Roeper

The worst gift that I ever gave a girl was a suitcase for Christmas. As in, 'I can't think of anything to give you, but here's a new suitcase.' Afterward, I was like, 'What were you thinking, idiot?'

Jensen Ackles

I'm a physicist, and we have something called Moore's Law, which says computer power doubles every 18 months. So every Christmas, we more or less assume that our toys and appliances are more or less twice as powerful as the previous Christmas.

Michio Kaku

For those, like me, who can't rely on being given a home smoker this Christmas, you can build your own approximation with just a roll of tin foil and a big wok or pan for which you have a lid.

Yotam Ottolenghi

Even today, I am still very child-like while designing. It's a bit like Christmas - each of your designs you create is like unravelling your presents.

Christian Louboutin

I am a Jew, and every single one of my ancestors was

Jewish. And it does not bother me even a little bit when people call those beautiful lit up, bejeweled trees Christmas trees. I don't feel threatened. I don't feel discriminated against.

Ben Stein

Godot is whatever it is in life that you are waiting for: 'I'm waiting to win the lottery. I'm waiting to fall in love'. For me, as a child, it was Christmas. At least that eventually came.

Ian Mckellen

With the song 'This Christmas' I wanted to do something that was kind of different. I mean, Donny Hathaway is an amazing artist. So I wanted to bring my flavor to the song so when people over the age of 45 or 50 hear it they'll be like 'OK, he did his thing with that record.' It's like I can appeal to everybody and not just a younger demographic.

Chris Brown

I love Christmas tree bulbs, and I started putting them in my paintings. You've got to plug this painting in, and it's got a rig in the back, so that each one can be replaced if it burns out.

David Lynch

I didn't know the full dimensions of forever, but I knew it was longer than waiting for Christmas to come.

Richard Brautigan

I'm bad on Valentine's Day, but even worse on Christmas. I go shopping at nine o'clock on December 24th every year. Nobody else is there. I'm in Toys'R'Us all by myself. I get there five minutes before closing.

Jamie Foxx

The holidays are my favorite time of year! Christmas was always one of the biggest celebrations in Sweden, and I look forward to the festivities each year.

Marcus Samuelsson

It's funny how we 'do' Christmas. Christmas is not something that we do, it is something that was done. It celebrates the long awaited arrival of the Messiah, Jesus Christ. We had nothing to do with it, but what we can do is praise God for the coming of the Lord, who washed away the sins of the world by dying on the cross.

Monica Johnson

Christmas comes during a season when the Earth is in its darkest time. It's a holiday for the family and for everyone.

Melissa Etheridge

My family makes these vinegars - out of everything from grapes to peaches and cherries. We go through the whole process with the giant vat and drainer, label them, and give them as Christmas presents.

Mario Batali

I remember wishing there was snow in L.A. And how jealous we used to get of those Christmas specials with kids playing in the snow.

Ice Cube

Comic-Con is nerd Christmas. People go wanting to have fun.

Chris Hardwick

The Christmas genre is a field that's been well-ploughed.

John Oates

According to an ancient Sardinian legend, the bodies of those who are born on Christmas Eve will never dissolve into dust but are preserved until the end of time.

Grazia Deledda

I'm a disorganized mess. My purse is gross: I once found a shoulder pad, string cheese, and a Christmas ornament in it!

Hoda Kotb

It may be a cliche, but it's true - the build-up to Christmas is so much more pleasurable than the actual day itself.

Julie Burchill

Orphans, dead parents, lonely children at Christmas, morose spoken word recordings, everything you love about the holidays. Move the turkey over so you can fit your head in the oven.

April Winchell

I love Christmas. I never used to. I didn't hate it, but I could take it or leave it. But, as I got to the age of 25 or 26, Christmas became quite a big deal, and I love it now. I love the food, and I love sharing time with people.

James McAvoy

I love Halloween, trick or treating and decorating the house. And I love Thanksgiving, because of the football and the fall weather. And of course, I love Christmas - that's my favorite of all!

Joe Nichols

I love Christmas. I really do love Christmas. I love being with my family and I love snow. I love the music and the lights and all of it.

Christina Applegate

My mother, she had a very good attitude toward money. I'm very grateful for the fact that we had to learn to save. I used to get like 50 pence a week, and I'd save it for like five months. And then I'd spend it on Christmas presents. I'd save up like eight pounds. It's nothing, but we did that.

Gemma Arterton

Like the Earth, the Web is a less appealing place than it used to be. If I want attitude and arguing and meanness and profanity and wrong information screamed at me as gospel, I'll get in a time machine and spend Christmas with my family in 1977.

J. R. Moehringer

I eat everything I want on Christmas day. I really don't watch what I eat. It's not like you have Christmas every day!

Adriana Lima

I went to Sunday School and liked the stories about Christ and the Christmas star. They were beautiful. They made you warm and happy to think about. But I didn't believe them.

Frances Farmer

Every July, I look forward to taping a Christmas show - in July in Nashville. In 98-degree weather. I love it.

Larry the Cable Guy

I was talking to one of my aunties at Christmas and she said she didn't think it was ever in my nature to go against the grain, that I was always a good boy. I think she was right - I did always want to be good.

James McAvoy

I think I'm a lot like other moms out there who feel like if we don't have the pecan pie we have every year, then it just won't be Christmas.

Faith Hill

We're raising our girls to understand the real meaning of Christmas, and to know that it's most important to have Christmas in your heart. We go to our local mall and donate toys, and we say prayers for all the people in the world who might not be as lucky as we are.

Faith Hill

I don't care why they love me, as long as they love me. I think people respect me because they feel like - I'm kind of like Christmas. I come back every year. You can't get rid of me. I just keep coming back.

David Hasselhoff

All families had their special Christmas food. Ours was called Dutch Bread, made from a dough halfway between bread and cake, stuffed with citron and every sort of nut from the farm - hazel, black walnut, hickory, butternut.

Paul Engle

For a long time all I wanted for Christmas were books about outdoor survival. I was convinced that the woods were calling me. I camped a lot, I took classes. At 18, I told myself if I don't live in the woods by myself by the time I'm 25, I have failed.

Chris Evans

Black Friday is not another bad hair day in Wall Street. It's the term used by American retailers to describe the day after the Thanksgiving Holiday, seen as the semi-official start of Christmas shopping season.

Evan Davis

When I was really young, I loved the movie 'White Christmas' - I still do - and I thought Rosemary Clooney was so pretty. When I was, like, nine, I would tell people, 'You know who I kind of look like? Rosemary Clooney.'

Tina Fey

The real reason Jews don't have more Hanukkah music is that, historically, American Jewish singer-songwriters were too busy making Christmas music. 'White Christmas,' 'Rudolph the Red-Nosed Reindeer,' 'Silver Bells' and 'The Christmas Song (Chestnuts Roasting)' were all written by Jews.

Matisyahu

A barn with cattle and horses is the place to begin Christmas; after all, that's where the original event happened, and that same smell was the first air that the Christ Child breathed.

Paul Engle

I still get up every morning at 4 A.M. I write seven days a week, including Christmas. And I still face a blank page every morning, and my characters don't really care how many books I've sold.

Dan Brown

I'm over the moon to be involved in the 'Doctor Who' Christmas special. I can't quite believe it as it's a part of the family tradition at the Jenkins household. I heard the news that I got the role on my 30th birthday and it was the best birthday present ever.

Katherine Jenkins

My family always makes a huge deal out of Christmas.

Jenna Morasca

Christmas was the one time of year when my brothers surfaced at home, when my parents and grandparents congregated to eat my mother's roast turkey.

Amanda Lindhout

The whole point of me doing a Christmas record and what I centered it around was the song 'Christmas with You' from the point-of-view of the soldiers in Iraq.

Rick Springfield

I write seven days a week, starting at 4 o'clock in the morning, including Christmas.

Dan Brown

We should celebrate Christmas throughout the year, but I believe the whole concept of giving was the basis of Christmas, that it was a charitable, you know, giving, and I think we got carried away with giving.

Victoria Osteen

Isn't that the great thing about Christmas? You get a lot of respite, time to recharge your batteries, time with family without too much else happening anywhere else in the world, time to focus on the people you love and the activities that you enjoy, time to exercise, to read.

Wayne Swan

My mother accidentally gave me food poisoning. She fed me baby carrots for a snack before Christmas dinner - but they had expired in June! I threw up for the next 24 hours.

Busy Philipps

When I was in seventh grade, I asked my parents for a mobile recording system for Christmas, and I got it. I didn't come out of my room for years after that. I'd get invited to the movies and I'd say, 'I'm gonna finish a couple of demos.'

Hunter Hayes

The No. 1 best-selling Christmas album of all time is from Kenneth Bruce Gorelick, the Jewish smooth-jazz legend Kenny G. American Jews have always produced a lot of holiday music, just not Hanukkah music.

Matisyahu

Kind 'Guardian' readers have been forwarding me round robin Christmas newsletters for years now: lengthy missives full of perfect children, exotic holidays, talented pets and endless, tedious detail. The notes that accompanied them revealed they had inspired in the original recipients everything from mild irritation to absolute rage.

Simon Hoggart

I got up one Christmas morning and we didn't have nothing to eat. We didn't have an apple, we didn't have an orange, we didn't have a cake, we didn't have nothing.

Muddy Waters

We never really had any kind of a Christmas. This is one part where my memory fails me completely.

Frank McCourt

Contemplating Christmas when you are isolated and far from home brings its own unique pain.

Amanda Lindhout

Christmas cookies can't help but be retro - they are memory first, sugar-flour-egg-redhot-gumdrop-sparkle reality second.

Dana Goodyear

I've got more than 600 pairs of Ray-Ban sunglasses, from 1950s originals to newer models. I have them on the wall like opticians do so I can pick out a pair that goes with my outfit. I had around 30 pairs, then my husband Rainer started getting them for me as birthday and Christmas gifts.

Suzi Quatro

When I was eight years old, I got a dummy for Christmas and started teaching myself. I got books and records and sat in front of the bathroom mirror, practising. I did my first show in the third grade and just kept going; there was no reason to quit.

Jeff Dunham

I wanted to have more songs with religious backgrounds. The Christmas record has strong, traditional hymns, but it also has a song called 'Christmas in Heaven' about missing someone that you love that's passed on, and wondering what's going on up there on Christmas.

Scotty McCreery

I read the Scriptures at the American Cathedral on Christmas and Easter; that's it. It's a task I love.

Olivia De Havilland

Well, the album 'Intuition' is out and just went platinum officially. So I think to have the music doing what it's doing right now, man, it's the ultimate. Nobody is really selling records out there but we are at a million records and we dropped it at Christmas, so we are just trying to get that thing to like two million, you know.

Jamie Foxx

Every day is like Halloween or Christmas eve for me. I go to bed, and I'm so excited to get back to work. I'm very lucky that I have a career like that 'cause not many people do.

Adam Green

We didn't have a whole lot of money when I was growing up either. I would always ask for magic books or magic tricks for my birthday or for Christmas and the rest of the year I either had to mow lawns or find part time jobs to help supplement the cost of doing magic.

Lance Burton

Music is my thing. It's my thing; it's what I love. It's what I do. It's football to me; it's Christmas to me; religion to me; poetry to me.

Ryan Adams

I used to sleep in the T-shirt I wore during the day and whatever ratty old gym shorts I could find on the floor. But one year for Christmas, someone gave me a very chic, comfortable pair of pajamas from Brooks Brothers, and I realized the error of my ways.

Derek Blasberg

I grew up poor, but I didn't really know it because of amazing places like the Salvation Army where we got a lot of our Christmas presents from.

Trey Songz

A simplified Christmas isn't about circumstances as much as it is about focus.

Ann Voskamp

Actually, my mother and Alfie came for three weeks' Christmas vacation and stayed for 21 years. I guess my mother never went back because she was lonely.

Frank McCourt

I love Christmas. Frosty the Snowman, peace on Earth and mangers, Salvation Army bell ringers and reindeer, the movie 'Meet Me in St. Louis,' office parties and cookies.

Mo Rocca

I stopped going to Kingdom Hall, the church, when I was 11 years old, so I was very young. They don't celebrate birthdays, you get no Christmas, so it's a very difficult religion for children to get into. And they do a lot of finger-pointing among the Jehovah's Witnesses.

Ja Rule

Yes, my first memory of singing, in general, was of a Christmas song. And then listening to Christmas music was really the first music I was ever connected to.

Christina Perri

It's hard and sometimes it's scary. It still amazes my mother. I went home for Christmas one year and there were fans all over the front lawn, hoping to see me.

Luke Perry

I actually share her view and understand her frustration when any government attempts to ban secular symbols like Santa Claus or Rudolph the Red Nose Reindeer or Christmas lights.

Steve Israel

No matter where I am in the world, I will always be back home for Christmas.

Malaika Arora Khan

Most Americans acquire dogs impulsively and for dubious reasons: as a Christmas gift for the kids. Because they saw one in a movie. To match the new living-room furniture. Because they moved to the suburbs and see a dog as part of the package.

Jon Katz

There's a lot of movies that aren't all about Christmas, or where Christmas isn't the focus, but have that spirit of Christmas in them. I love that sequence in 'Auntie Mame,' where she's in the department store, sewing at Macy's, and she doesn't know how to do anything but fill out a form as 'cash on delivery!'

Robert Osborne

In 1934, the American Jewish charities offered to find homes for 300 German refugee children. We were on the SS Washington, bound for New York, Christmas 1934.

Jack Steinberger

I want to go to Lapland and see Father Christmas, and now I've got a child, so I've got an excuse. Also, I'd like to go to South America especially as I'm now living in that part of the world, in L.A. now. And I must get down to Mexico.

Ashley Jensen

In the spring of 1994 I decided not to seek reelection to the Senate. I had made the decision 12 years earlier, Christmas Day of 1982, just after I had been first elected to a full term, that I would do the best I could for a limited time.

George J. Mitchell

I was 23 when I learned how to cook; I grew up around the same time. It was precisely then that Thanksgiving started to mean something more. Growing up, Christmas was always about me, and eventually you, when I finally started to enjoy the giving part. But Thanksgiving is always about us.

Rosecrans Baldwin

I had eight brothers and sisters. Every Christmas my

younger brother Bobby would wake up extra early and open everybody's presents - everybody's - so by the time the rest of us got up, all the gifts were shredded, ribbons off, torn open and thrown aside.

Tommy Hilfiger

A Christmas Carol is such a fool-proof story you can't louse it up.

Leonard Maltin

Whatever he does should be seen as working at the Presidency and if he goes to Colorado for Christmas, it should be for a minimum amount of time, the family tradition and family get-together aspect emphasized, and it be seen as a working vacation.

Robert Teeter

Christmas is a huge thing in my family. We usually start decorating the day after Thanksgiving. We spend Christmas Eve with one set of grandparents, and Christmas Day with the other grandparents and our family.

Samantha Isler

It felt very natural to me to write a Christmas song, but at the same time I had to really put all sorts of pressure aside and just let the creativity flow and see what came out.

Christina Perri

Every Christmas, all around Ghana, there are tons of these parties and they are full of everything that exists in human life in Ghana and worldwide.

Taiye Selasi

Now, a lot of what we are doing right now, quite frankly, is because of what happened on Christmas. Many of the things were kind of in the works. We were already planning, for example, the purchase and deployment of advanced imaging technology. You call them body scanners. We call them AITs (Advanced Imaging Technologies).

Janet Napolitano

My earliest, most impactful encounter with a book was when I was seven and awoke early on Christmas morning to find Roald Dahl's 'Charlie and the Chocolate Factory' in my stocking. I had never been so excited by the sight of a book - and have possibly never been since!

Sophie Kinsella

It's funny, I was talking to somebody who writes for a cop show, and he was saying how they aren't allowed to acknowledge Christmas, Thanksgiving, Valentine's Day, just because it has to be able to play forever.

Hannah Simone

I love presents, But since I've gotten older, I haven't really wanted anything. Christmas is about family.

Jacob Latimore

The term 'natural resources' confuses people. 'Natural resources' are not like a finite number of gifts under the Christmas tree. Nature is given, but resources are created.

Alex Tabarrok

I'm well-travelled so I can see places coming up. I went to St. Croix in the West Indies at Christmas and it had been hit by a really bad tornado. Values there have gone down but I guarantee they will be up again in eight years. So I'll get in now while it's cheap as chips.

Melanie Brown

I'd just got back from filming my role as Flo in 'Kidnap & Ransom' when I got the news that Channel 4 had re-commissioned 'Fresh Meat,' so I think it was the first Christmas I could actually relax knowing that I had three months' work sorted. As an actor, that's always a good feeling.

Kimberley Nixon

Throughout my teenage years, I read 'A Christmas Carol' by Charles Dickens every December. It was a story that never failed to excite me, for as well as being a Dickens enthusiast, I have always loved ghost stories.

John Boyne

Every year, like a good Catholic, I wait for Christmas. Putting up the lights, decorating the tree, making sweets and then unwrapping gifts on Christmas morning... it's a tradition my family has followed since I was very little.

Malaika Arora Khan

I'm so depressed. Christmas is the worst of all. Holidays are terrible, worse than Sundays. I get melancholia.

David O. Selznick

I started DJing, breakdancing and MCing in the '70s and I got my record deal in 1979 with 'Christmas Rap.'

Kurtis Blow

I make personal appearances around the country. I'm starting a book tour now, and I may be coming to Toronto with the Learning Annex, which I'm doing all through the United States, so that may come up just before Christmas.

Burt Ward

I think it's important not to grow up too fast. I'm 26 now, and I still can't wait for Christmas Day. The inner seven-year-old isn't buried too deeply in me.

Laura Haddock

In our racist, sexist society, Christmas is the eight hours when we stop killing each other and gratuitous overeating is encouraged so that the starving and other people in the world can die!

Lloyd Kaufman

My younger brother will remember that he received a transistor radio for Christmas. I took it apart and it never worked again.

Stephen Elop

I don't want to see people decorating a house or digging a garden. As for guys like Jonathan Ross, he got an award there last Christmas. What for? He doesn't sing, dance or tell jokes, does he?

Ian St. John

Christmas is a season which almost all Christians observe in one way or another. Some keep it as a religious season. Some keep it as a holiday. But all over the world, wherever there are Christians, in one way or another Christmas is kept.

J. C. Ryle

No sane local official who has hung up an empty stocking over the municipal fireplace, is going to shoot Santa Claus just before a hard Christmas.

Al Smith

I wouldn't recommend young kids see 'Speedway Junkie.'
It's definitely an age-appropriate movie - dark and realistic
and edgy. If young kids want to see me, go see the
Christmas movie.

Jonathan Taylor Thomas

One of my favorite movies of all time is 'It's A Wonderful
Life,' which is a pretty interesting choice for a seasonal
Christmas favorite, because it's about a guy who wants to
commit suicide and is presented with reasons not to.

Frank Darabont

At school, there was an annual school disco and I'd be
standing in my bedroom wondering what to wear for hours
on end. Eventually I'd arrive at a decision that was just the
most ridiculous costume you could have ever devised - I
think it was probably knitted Christmas jumpers on top of
buttoned-up white shirts.

Guy Berryman

There's always been something a little pathetic for me at

the work parties I've attended, especially thinking back to the restaurants I worked in. I remember a Christmas party in which we all got free T-shirts with the restaurant on the front and our names on the back.

Said Sayrafiezadeh

Every Christmas now for years, I have found myself wondering about the point of the celebration. As the holiday has become more ecumenical and secular, it has lost much of the magic that I remember so fondly from childhood.

Whitley Strieber

In fact, I was one of the few trusted people that Lucy allowed to play with their kids. I spent time at their summer home, rode horses at their ranch, and swam at their beach house. I even spent a Christmas with them at Palm Springs one year.

Keith Thibodeaux

Christmas movies, it's a hard thing to do. The danger is you just end up with a Hollywood star with a Santa beard. You risk it being fake and cheesy and not real.

Peter Baynham

Seeing the actual, 'The Chronicles of Narnia: The Lion, the Witch, and the Wardrobe', I absolutely loved it. It became one of my favorite films. It was a real Christmas classic and it was one of the most popular films ever in British history. So I think if someone told me that I'd be part of the franchise, then I would have thought they were mad.

Will Poulter

I loved rock and roll when that came in, Bill Haley, Little Richard, Fats Domino, Buddy Holly, Elvis Presley, all those great records. So I begged my mom and dad for a guitar, which eventually they did get me for Christmas, but it went out of tune very quickly, and it hurt my fingers.

Ian McLagan

Throughout my college years, I'd watch my sister squeal every Christmas as she unwrapped another 'Buffy' DVD set. I didn't know much about the series, but I was filled with that obnoxious self-importance that comes from having decided to be an Academic Who Reads Serious Things.

Marie Rutkoski

Like my best friend, I asked for drums for Christmas, and got them. But when he moved on to guitar, I realized two things: (1) guitar is a much more expressive instrument, (2) way more girls pay attention to guitar players than to drummers.

Greg Iles

If you're an English actor, and you're asked to do an episode - especially the Christmas episode - of 'Downton Abbey,' you can't turn it down. It's like, 'Of course!'

Janet Montgomery

I might do 'X Factor' next year. It's looking good that I won't get the sack at Christmas.

Gary Barlow

I'm totally the 'decorate early, start listening to Christmas songs super early' guy. I've just always been that way.

Drake Bell

I intend to keep writing Christmas songs. There's still a lot more about Christmas that can be captured and feel like old-time Christmas. A lot of the traditions haven't been explained in song.

Clint Black

With a track like 'White Christmas,' everybody has done that song in every format you can imagine, so I just looked at the chords at that particular song and what chords would make it work. That's kind of quite a sad song, and I had this idea of someone singing it in the subway, someone who is homeless, old and sad.

Vince Clarke

Christmas really is about all the cliches: health, happiness and love. A future with my family is the important thing... to stay alive for them.

Sylvie Meis

I'm one of those people who had Christmas and my birthday always combined, and generally, my birthday was pretty much ignored. But my parents are always good about making some kind of special effort to make me feel like I also have a birthday that exists.

Noel Wells

I'd have to say, for me, as a child, my favorite memories were always centered around Christmas time. It always seemed like no matter how much money my parents had or didn't have, we got completely spoiled rotten. There were always presents under the tree, and we always did special things, like hide elves around the house.

Josie Bissett

Certainly, nothing would stop me coming home for Christmas, if I can. But I've worked a lot in theatre, and in theatre in New York, we work Christmas Day a lot of the time as well.

Brian F. O'Byrne

I'd rather do community service than sit and write a load of Christmas cards.

Paul O'Grady

You can't allow the forces of political correction to shut you up. I mean, why are people afraid to say, 'Merry Christmas?' Give me a break. If people don't like it, yeah, they can go do something else.

Benjamin Carson

Tiny quails may not seem as impressive as a mammoth turkey, but there is something refreshing about a spread of individual birds on the Christmas table.

Yotam Ottolenghi

I've always been shy, but I see that as a good thing because it kept me focused on music. When I was in seventh grade, I asked my parents for a mobile recording system for Christmas, and I got it. I didn't come out of my room for years after that. I'd get invited to the movies and I'd say, 'I'm gonna finish a couple of demos.'

Hunter Hayes

Christmas means a great deal to me. I was reared in a family that celebrated Christmas to some extent, but I married into a family that celebrated Christmas in a big way. And my wife always made a big thing of Christmas for the children. We have five children, and we had a terrific time at Christmas.

Billy Graham

There would be no Christmas if there was no Easter.

Gordon B. Hinckley

I was at the vice president's Christmas party. I thought that his speech was spectacular, and I knew that it was a very emotional and difficult thing for him to do, but I admonished him for not waiting just one more stinking day.

Bradley Whitford

Making a Christmas album is looked upon by some people as the thing you do when you are heading towards retirement.

Annie Lennox

You are not practicing Judaism if you celebrate Christmas.

Elliott Abrams

A Christian's celebration of Christmas should be a lot different from that of nonbelievers.

Monica Johnson

During the holiday season, Christmas specifically, it can be hard to be away from family and friends.

Monica Johnson

The Swedish Christmas is definitely unique, even throughout Scandinavia. Like Christmas everywhere, it's a very family-centered holiday.

Marcus Samuelsson

There's been a concerted effort to steal Christmas.

Jerry Falwell

It kills me when people talk about California hedonism. Anybody who talks about California hedonism has never spent a Christmas in Sacramento.

Joan Didion

Christmas is the antithesis of Thanksgiving. Christmas is pretty much a man-made holiday.

John Clayton

Christmas in L.A. is weird. There's no snow. It's not even cold.

Ellie Goulding

I can't tell you how scary it can be walking onto a movie and suddenly joining this family, it's like going to somebody else's Christmas dinner, everyone knows everyone, and you're there and you're not quite sure what you're supposed to be doing.

John Cleese

Christmas is a Christian holiday, and any self-respecting person of another religion should not celebrate a holiday that they don't believe in. Clearly, Christ is in the name of the holiday, so there should be a belief in Him.

Monica Johnson

Fragrance is a very personal gift, and I think that's why it makes a great Christmas gift. There's a very distinct signature to it, so if you give it as a gift, I like to think that it's from a person that thinks very highly of you.

Ryan Reynolds

I always liked it when people go back in time to discover things about themselves, like with 'A Christmas Carol' and you're getting a tour of your life by the ghosts of Christmas past, present and future.

John Cusack

From a commercial point of view, if Christmas did not exist it would be necessary to invent it.

Katharine Whitehorn

I don't know if anybody's ever ready for another award season. It's kind of like Christmas.

James McAvoy

The Christmas market at the Barcelona Cathedral sells all kinds of things for your Nativity scene. It will also give you a good idea of Catalan culture.

Jose Andres Puerta

I made a French film called 'Merry Christmas' which is a very European film. It's a World War I piece.

Diane Kruger

So we're considering doing a new Christmas album, because there's been Christmas episodes since then, and maybe finally do the version of 'The Most Offensive Song Ever' with lyrics intact.

Trey Parker

In my adolescence, I think I felt very outcast; I felt lonely. I felt great loneliness, and sometimes I wouldn't partake in Christmas, and I would go off and wander in the streets of Melbourne.

Michael Leunig

Don't give me books for Christmas; I already have a book.

Jean Harlow

Tax cuts should be for life, not just for Christmas.

George Osborne

The pattern of a newspaperman's life is like the plot of 'Black Beauty.' Sometimes he finds a kind master who gives him a dry stall and an occasional bran mash in the form of a Christmas bonus, sometimes he falls into the hands of a mean owner who drives him in spite of spavins and expects him to live on potato peelings.

A. J. Liebling

I used to have nightmares when I was a little kid that I woke up prematurely and opened all the Christmas presents. And then I would be so relieved when I woke up and I realized that I hadn't done it.

Claire Danes

One Christmas build-up tradition, however, has totally bypassed me - that of going up to town and 'doing a show.'

Julie Burchill

In my experience, those who make the biggest fuss about not spending much at Christmas are generally the ones who buy what they want and eat where they want 12 months a year.

Julian Baggini

It's quite a famous story that takes place on Christmas Eve, and the Germans, French, and Scottish are trying to make peace one night and they bury their dead and they play football. I play a German opera singer, in German, which I never have so I am really excited about that.

Diane Kruger

The way my family always did Christmas was on Christmas Eve, it wasn't really centered around a dinner on Christmas Eve. It was more about keeping the kids calm. Sometime after dark is when we were going to open all the presents underneath the tree from Mom, Dad and the kids and everything - just the family presents was every Christmas Eve.

Blake Shelton

I've been playing on Christmas for the last 10, 11, 12 years. So just got to get up early with the babies, and give them their toys and try to get a nap in and just come to play.

Shaquille O'Neal

Atheists well understand that Christmas is the most visible display of religion in the world, and that any diminishment of it is a good thing to militant secularists.

Bill O'Reilly

For a Jewish guy, I've recorded a lot of Christmas albums.

Barry Manilow

I think it's kind of difficult to write a good Christmas song because you have a narrow framework of references that you have to work within, and at the same time you want to do something that's personally original and hopefully somewhat unique.

John Oates

My first real job, I sold Christmas trees when I was twelve for extra money. I did that until I was fifteen. Then I bagged groceries, and I worked at the first Borders ever in Tulsa, Oklahoma.

Bill Hader

The denominational world tries to pressure its members to focus on the birth of Christ, but in doing so layers of guilt are imposed, and competition gets complicated as one Christmas program tries to outdo the other.

John Clayton

I grew up asking for everything under the sun for Christmas, but I knew I wasn't going to get it all.

Faith Hill

Once you start a business, you have to grow it and grow with it - starting a business is not just for Christmas.

Natalie Massenet

I like animals. I like people who like animals. I hate people who love animals to the point they lose their sense of reason. I'm talking the 'my computer wallpaper is my dog,' 'I hang a Christmas stocking for my cat' crowd.

John Ridley

'Make your plate look like a Christmas tree,' I tell people, 'mostly green with splashes of other bright colors.'

Victoria Moran

Somehow we just don't make the same boisterous fun of Holy Week that we do of Christmas. No one plans to have a holly, jolly Easter.

Frederica Mathewes-Green

My parents still treat Christmas like I'm thirteen years old.

Mike Shinoda

'The Nightmare Before Christmas' is my number one biggest influence artistically in every way.

Amy Lee

It was, you know, probably 80 degrees out in L.A., and my dad took me outside and there was snow. At the time, I thought, 'Every kid doesn't have snow in their backyard on Christmas?'

Tori Spelling

My mom is a really good cook. I didn't get the cooking gene, but she cooks this really amazing dinner every Christmas, and that's always really fun.

Miranda Cosgrove

It can't be overstated how wonderful it is not to have to

audition any more. Any actor will tell you, it's like Christmas.

Bill Nighy

I was a postman one Christmas and I developed a morbid fear of dogs.

Diane Abbott

Most of the soap operas always use the Christmas special to kill huge quantities of their characters. So they have trams coming off their rails, or cars slamming into each other or burning buildings. It's a general clean-out.

Julian Fellowes

We go to Italy every winter, and my husband's mother has a bingo party on Christmas. Every woman brings a dish: lentils, cavolo nero, tons of beans, polenta, every type of cheese, bruschetta, fresh vegetables, and local olive oil and wine.

Debi Mazar

I am one of those people who is not very patient in the

makeup chair. I have been offered movies like 'Planet of the Apes' and stuff like 'The Grinch Who Stole Christmas' and I turned them down.

John C. Reilly

Every Christmas should begin with the sound of bells, and when I was a child mine always did. But they were sleigh bells, not church bells, for we lived in a part of Cedar Rapids, Iowa, where there were no churches.

Paul Engle

We no longer sing and dance. We don't know how to. Instead, we watch other people sing and dance on the television screen. Christmas, which was once a festival of active enjoyment, has turned into a binge of purely passive pleasures.

Tom Hodgkinson

So many people release albums before Christmas and they get lost in the Christmas rush.

Bonnie Tyler

Songs that aren't even remotely connected to Christmas are now officially canonized Christmas tunes. 'Frosty the Snowman,' 'Jingle Bells' and 'Winter Wonderland' never mention anything religious but are still notches in Christmas' belt of musical dominance.

Matisyahu

I love cooking during Christmas, all smells like the hot apple cider, the hot spiced wine.

Amy Smart

Easter may seem boring to children, and it is blessedly unencumbered by the silly fun that plagues Christmas. Yet it contains the one thing needful for every human life: the good news of Resurrection.

Frederica Mathewes-Green

He put a ring in the toe of a stocking. On Christmas Eve, we opened our stockings and it was there at the bottom of the toe. Then he got down on his knees and he was shaking.

Kyra Sedgwick

It's more like Christmas, you know, when you get a shot in that looks great and it's exactly what you want. It's a great feeling, and there's nothing like it.

Zack Snyder

My first job, 9 years old, part-time, was selling Christmas cards door-to-door. Ten years old, my brother and I had paper routes. We delivered a morning paper called the 'L.A. Examiner.' Get up at 4 o'clock, fold your papers, deliver them and get ready for school.

John Paul DeJoria

Every singer eventually gets around to a Christmas disc.

Renee Fleming

Is it possible Hanukkah doesn't inspire folksy songs? Plot lines may be a part. The Christmas story has a lot of material to work with. There's Jesus and his birth, the wise men, their gifts and tons of frankincense.

Matisyahu

Felixstowe, the United Kingdom's largest port, stops work

only for Christmas Day and for crane-toppling Force 9 gales.

Rose George

I remember being banned from other houses as a younger child during the winter holiday season; I was the only one who didn't believe in Santa Claus, and I was ruining everyone's Christmas.

Jami Attenberg

I think we felt the pressure more at first than this time around. But still you don't want to let anyone down. I never even met Patrick until we had a Christmas party at Ian McKellen's house on the first movie and then I didn't see him again until the premiere.

Rebecca Romijn

When I was five my parents bought me a ukulele for Christmas. I quickly learned how to play it with my father's guidance. Thereafter, my father regularly taught me all the good old fashioned songs.

Tony Visconti

One of the best Christmas presents I ever got was the globe that I now keep right beside my desk.

Tess Gerritsen

The vocal arrangements are a big part of the formula for a Bad Religion song - layered harmonies and background vocals. So when I start to describe the elements of Bad Religion's sound, it starts to sound like a Christmas choir.

Greg Graffin

I love 'White Christmas.' That's one of my favorites just because I love the music. I love the story, Bing Crosby. It's just one of my all time favorites. And it's hard to have a Christmas without seeing a little bit of Jimmy Stewart and angels running around town.

Scott Bakula

'A Christmas Carol' has been described as the most perfect of Dickens's works and as a quintessential heart-warming story, and it is certainly the most popular.

Claire Tomalin

The Christmas story has such power and such appeal every year. There are other stories we get tired of. You think of your favorite movie; you don't want to watch it 15 times.

Frederica Mathewes-Green

I'm Jewish and my wife isn't so right now we're literally decorating a Christmas tree with Jewish stars draped around it.

Max Greenfield

I never really did Christmas before. Christmas Day? I mean - what's that? What's it all about? I was always flying on Christmas Day.

Monica Seles

'A Christmas Story' is my favorite Christmas movie.

Paul Pierce

I think 'Elf' is funny, with Will Ferrell. That's a great Christmas movie.

Robert Osborne

I was lucky enough to grow up in a home where I woke up Christmas morning and had toys. I know that's not the case with all people and I don't think kids should go without experiencing that sort of joy.

Lucy Hale

One Christmas I had no money, and so I went home and just, like, wrote a poem; I mean, I didn't write them, but I just handed out poems as Christmas presents. Like, 'Here's a Pablo Neruda poem that really made me think of you.'

June Diane Raphael

A lot of sequins for New Year's! Red, green, white - I fail at all of that because I'm always in black. But for Christmas, I do love wearing cute dresses with tights and a pair of boots.

Ashley Benson

Like my dad, I have a Christmas party most years. I like to celebrate and see as many people as possible.

Lauren Graham

The unfortunate thing about working for yourself is that you have the worst boss in the world. I work every day of the year except at Christmas, when I work a half day.

David Eddings

I hate to say it, but Christmas as a kid was always a moneymaking venture for me. I played trumpet, and a friend of mine who played trombone and a guy who played tuba, every Christmas we'd go out for three or four days beforehand and play Christmas carols on our horns.

John Tesh

From a very young age, I liked to take apart things. All of my Christmas gifts would wind up in a million pieces. I actually recall taking apart my dad's lawnmower three times to understand how combustible engines work.

Homaro Cantu

We always had lutefisk for Christmas dinner, after which Dad read from the Norwegian Bible.

Peter Agre

I like, 'I Believe In Father Christmas' - that is one of my favorites it is a lovely composition; 'Colder Than Winter' as well. There are so many beautiful songs.

Sarah Brightman

I've taught fifth-year Christmas leavers last thing on a Friday afternoon. Basically, if you can face that you can face anything.

Johann Lamont

I just travel all the time. And I was just looking at the schedules now and starting the first week of October I will be every weekend with somebody at tournaments through Christmas. So it gets very difficult to just go away and not do that.

Ivan Lendl

One Christmas my father kept our tree up till March. He hated to see it go. I loved that.

Mo Rocca

Fantastic! Right in the middle of that long stretch between Christmas and Spring Break, your coats are getting dirty, everything's dark, dingy - what a great time for a movie!

John Hughes

I was thrilled one year when I was younger when not only did my brothers get hockey sticks for Christmas - but I did too!

Nancy Kerrigan

I loved the first Christmas I had in England.

Blythe Danner

I grew up with the classics. My mom and I would sit and watch 'Singin' in the Rain' and 'White Christmas' - those kind of movies.

Lucas Grabeel

Mom still has a huge, beautifully decorated Christmas tree. The whole family comes together after midnight mass and has the traditional plum cake and wine. We spend the night at mom's home, and in the morning we wake up and open the presents. In the afternoon, we sit down to have a traditional Christmas lunch.

Malaika Arora Khan

Yep, I'm a geek. Ever since I got the Millennium Falcon for Christmas in 1978. And I still have it, in perfect condition, just without the box... but I still play with it!

Joseph Gatt

My first publication was a haiku in a children's magazine when I was 9 years old. I received one dollar for it! I gave the check to my dad for Christmas, and he framed it and hung it over his desk.

Linda Sue Park

You know, I started my career in politics in 1967. I'm not new to this. I did not just fall off the Christmas tree. I understand the world is complex. I know that there are people out there who want to hurt other people.

Dennis Kucinich

Being half Jewish, we grew up with Christmas trees but

had Jewish ornaments.

Gina Rodriguez

In our racist, sexist society, Christmas is the 8 hours when we stop killing each other and gratutious over eating is encouraged so that the starving and other people in the world can die!

Lloyd Kaufman

Christmas albums are not something you do frequently.

Isaac Hanson

There are very few people who have done more than one Christmas album.

Isaac Hanson

I really like the European carols, and I like that captivating sound that they have that isn't usually in Christmas songs.

David Archuleta

'The war in Iraq - if Osama was a Christian - it's the Christmas present he never would have expected.

Michael Scheuer

For many of us, Christmas lunch is the most special meal of the year - and I certainly want nothing but the very best for this celebration.

Sheherazade Goldsmith

But Tammy Faye calls me, and Ron Jeremy calls me, Erik Estrada sends me a Christmas card every year.

Trishelle Cannatella

I love the excess of Christmas. The shopping season that begins in September, the bad pop star recordings of Christmas carols, the decorations that don't know when to come down.

Mo Rocca

I think the people who are making Christmas-themed movies today feel that people are more cynical about Christmas. There's more of an edge.

Leonard Maltin

I'd like to do a Christmas album. I've never done a Christmas album.

Tanya Tucker

I got a guitar when I was about 14, for a Christmas present, and went from there.

Robin Trower

I put the copy of 'A Christmas Carol' that my grandfather had first read to me 60 years ago on my desk, and I began to write. The result, for better or for worse, is the 'Christmas Spirits.' I plan to read it to my grandson.

Whitley Strieber

I hate feeling full, so Christmas is about the only time I really stuff myself.

Rupert Penry-Jones

Adults are tempted to produce and perform Christmas for

their kids and their families, and they arrive at Christmas Day weary and disillusioned.

Ann Voskamp

I love all the gift guides that the magazines put out, whether it's 'InStyle' doing Mother's Day gifts or color guides, or the 'O' magazine Christmas guide.

Dylan Lauren

My Christmas present to myself each year is to see how much air travel can open up the world and take me to places as far from sheltered California and Japan as possible.

Pico Iyer

I'm not going to put out a Christmas CD until it's coming out of me naturally.

TobyMac

People have nannies and big cars, and they want to go to Maui for Christmas. When there are those kind of stakes involved, people get ruthless.

Amy Sherman-Palladino

During the holidays, everyone needs a break from studying for exams and Christmas shopping. I wanted to put together a diverse tour that rocks in many musical directions but always points to Christ.

TobyMac

South Park started as a little video Christmas card.

Joel Hodgson

I grew up as a photo nut. Every Christmas I would get a new camera. It's a huge part of my life.

Kevin Systrom

Without social networks, you're not the coolest thing on the Christmas list, and you're not getting any bite.

Joe Green

May I share with you my earliest memory of a political row? It was with my mother, about the Queen - classic

Freudian stuff, shrinks would say. I was eight, and refusing to watch the Queen's Christmas Day broadcast.

Alastair Campbell

Grief is a room without doors - but somehow, with its tinsel and cliches, Christmas finds a way in.

Simon Van Booy

I got this Christmas gift with the entire Beatles catalog. I had fun trying to duplicate what I was hearing on these records, only using the instruments I had at hand - an acoustic guitar, and that's all. It was endlessly amusing to me to try to imitate John Lennon and Paul McCartney's harmonies using the guitar.

M. Ward

I played guitar from the age of four or five. Every year there would be a slightly larger triangular box under the Christmas tree, until finally I got one that was big enough to make a proper sound.

Johnny Marr

The next thing I wrote was in a writing class at night school. It was about a poor woman who worked at a dime store and who was all alone for Christmas in Laurel, Mississippi.

Beth Henley

To me, the most important thing is to wear something that I love and feel comfortable in, and Christmas is a great opportunity to get one of my old favourites out.

Amber Le Bon

When I was eight, my mum found me humming to myself and scribbling on a scrap of paper. When she asked me what I was doing, I got shy. I was writing a Christmas song, and I had never shared my music with anyone before. Reluctantly, I sang it for her... and she loved it. Of course she did - she's my mum.

Neil Jackson

And of course there's so much music in and around our family. I had a piano during Christmas because it's obviously useful through the season. There are so many people, songwriters, who are around.

Ashley Judd

From the time that I can remember, I worked to make money - either baby-sitting, or one year wrapping gifts at a department store at Christmas, so I could have my own money.

Christie Hefner

I've been in elementary education for years and my belief is that Christmas pageants in schools are little more than conditioning kids for the Christian religion.

Jack Bowman

Did you know that Christmas Day is absolutely the best day to fly? It is. No crowded airports and crowded planes. I always flew to Australia. That's what Christmas was for me - a plane journey to the next tournament.

Monica Seles

I absolutely adore Agatha Christie; so much so that when I received a kitten for my Christmas present, I called her Agatha, and I already have a cat called Hercule!

Kimberley Nixon

A friend gave me a CD of the 'Pathetique' Symphony as a Christmas present. I went home, and I put on the CD expecting to listen to Tchaikovsky. But it started 'ta ta ta taaa.' It was too long for me. I didn't understand it at first, but then I fell in love, in love, in love.

Gustavo Dudamel

Christmas was always a big holiday in our family. Every Christmas Eve before we'd go to bed, my mom and dad would read to us two or three stories and they would always be 'The Happy Prince,' 'The Gift of the Magi' and 'Twas the Night Before Christmas,' and I would like to keep that alive.

Cameron Mathison

I really want a Christmas in New York one year, when it's snowing. Like, it's Christmas morning, and you have a fight with someone, and you run down the street, and it's snowing, and you can't find them.

Courtney Barnett

I love all things Christmas.

Samantha Barks

It's fun when you start a movie, because it's kind of like you get to go Christmas shopping... you get to make your wish list and you start thinking about what each character needs.

Spike Jonze

It will be a hard game if you think about winning a championship. We need to think about our own game at the moment and focus on getting good results especially over the Christmas period.

Dennis Bergkamp

Yeah, I started when I was 6 years old. My brother and sister would get all of these presents at Christmas time from the cast and crew of their show and I was jealous. So I decided that I had to become an actor.

Sara Gilbert

Windows are as essential to office prestige as Christmas is to retailing.

Enid Nemy

I worked every day - Christmas Eve, birthdays - trying to become a great basketball player. Everywhere I went, I had a basketball.

Harvey Mason, Jr.

A typical Christmas is me shucking oysters. I love them and I always get them in at Christmas.

Hugh Bonneville

I got my first instrument for Christmas when I was three or four years old. My parents got me a mandolin because it was the only instrument that would fit me because I was so small. I went straight from that into the drums when I was six, and then I started playing guitar when I was seven or eight.

Chord Overstreet

Lately I did a film called All I Want for Christmas and it was well received. This gave me a new point of view and a new respect for my work as an actress.

Sarah Polley

My father died when I was young and I was raised by my grandmother, Emma Klonjlaleh Brown. We could afford to eat chicken just once a year, on Christmas.

George Weah

So many Christmas films either are twee, or try and go super edgy, then stick on something Christmassy at the end of the movie.

Peter Baynham

I'm a strong nonbeliever in the Christmas letter where you don't really read it because it's just full of kind of meaningless information. It doesn't really resonate to the person reading it, but it means so much to the person that wrote it.

BD Wong

Chum was a British boy's weekly which, at the end of the year was bound into a single huge book; and the following Christmas parents bought it as Christmas presents for male children.

A. E. van Vogt

Well, because I have twin seven-year-old boys, I enjoy the gift giving stuff a great deal. We do both Hanukkah and Christmas, so it is a costly, though extremely pleasing proposition.

Fred Melamed

I hate Christmas, really. I don't really give presents away or expect any.

Joy Bryant

Then, when I got in the military, I used to host - even in high school - I hosted the talent shows, and when I was in the military I would host all of our base Christmas parties and stuff.

Gary Owens

I realised that you could easily turn any room into a cinema with a projector, so I went on and on at my parents for one. They eventually got me a projector for Christmas when I was ten, and I realised I'd made a ridiculous mistake - I'd forgotten to say 'movie' projector; I got a still one.

Kevin Brownlow

I don't think of Home Depot as romantic, but I do think the Christmas wonderland they put up during the holidays is magical. That is what Home Depot is to me, and that is the only romantic thing about it.

Betty Who

I got my first instrument at Christmas when I was three or four. My dad and mom got me a mandolin. It was the only instrument that fit me because I was so small. I went straight from that into drums when I was six and then started playing guitar when I was seven or eight.

Chord Overstreet

'White Christmas' is one of my favorite movies, so I've always just had a love for that kind of golden era musical.

Jessie Mueller

One of my favorite times of year is around Christmas when my entire family gets together and we make tamales together. It's a full two-day event, and we create an assembly line. It's awesome because everyone has his or her own part in making the dish. It's so much fun.

Sabrina Bryan

For Christmas I do gift bags for my friends and the cast, and I put 'treat yo self' key chains in there. And people send me pictures of 'treat yo self' all the time.

Retta

Part of me wants to be married and have everybody around the table for Christmas. But when you're married, your life becomes integrated solely with that person. There are too many characters running around inside me. Maybe they should all be married to somebody different.

Cindy Williams

I owe my life to my father. I remember that my first Christmas present was a ball. In the district where we lived, there weren't many kids who had one.

Sergio Aguero

I'm not a fan of musicals at all, but I do think 'The Nightmare Before Christmas' is a very good. I always thought 'Walk the Line' was very good, too. I was in 'Nowhere Boy.' I played Paul McCartney. That was kind of musical - we did songs in that.

Thomas Sangster

'Joker' was a violent, dark, and brutal book, so I wanted to do something a little less heavy. I played around with the idea of a children's book, and that eventually became 'Noel.' And I just kept finding these parallels between things I could do with Batman and Charles Dickens' 'A Christmas Carol.'

Lee Bermejo

I do love Christmas, although my wife puts me to shame. She is a huge Christmas fan, so we do love us some Christmas in our house.

Sebastian Arcelus

My very first acting role was Tiny Tim in 'A Christmas Carol.'

Leland Orser

The South has a way of worshipping appearances - the suburbs are all about presentation and amazing flowers and a beautiful yard and dinner parties that impress people and having the Christmas lights just right.

Paul Downs Colaizzo

I grew up playing games, and I remember Christmas 1981 when my dad got us an Intellivision, and we all sat around and played 'Astrosmash' for hours on end. It was a big part of my youth.

Roger Craig Smith

If you look at Christmas movies, there are certain things in them that lend themselves to a 'Harold & Kumar' movie. In particular, the more out-of-this-world things like Santa Claus and flying reindeer.

Hayden Schlossberg

Our family's special holiday tradition is going over to my grandparent's house on Christmas morning. My grandma cooks a big breakfast, and I love hearing her tell old funny stories.

Caroline Sunshine

My family background is Mexican, and I was born in Chicago. It's pretty much family tradition every time we get together for Christmas and major holidays to sing. Our family time is centered around the food and a little bit of performing for one another.

Ailyn Perez

I think that it's fun to get the script and open it like a Christmas present. That's 'Alcatraz' or anything that I'm working on. If the groundwork has been laid too much, the surprises aren't there.

Jeffrey Pierce

I became hugely overweight and then hated myself because it was a form of self-abuse, something over which I had no control. I think the thing compulsive over-eaters want to achieve is that stuffed-full Christmas afternoon feeling.

Marcus Brigstocke

First of all, I've been having a wonderful run of luck with cover albums, songs I didn't write. I had five pop cover albums and two Christmas albums, and they were all very successful.

Barry Manilow

I know a lot of actors picture themselves winning Academy Awards. I really just wanted to do a Christmas movie because it's the kind of movie that I really love to watch. I'm a sucker for the holidays.

Leigh-Allyn Baker

For Christmas every year, my mother used to give me those cheap little diaries that would tell your horoscope and provide a little blank slot for each day.

Patti Smith

Fashion Week is like Christmas.

Brad Goreski

The cheese board is my big treat at Christmas that I have to deny myself during the rest of year.

Johnny Vegas

I beg people not to accept the seasonal ritual of well-timed charity on Christmas Eve. It's blasphemy.

Jonathan Kozol

In France, Christmas is a family holiday. You stay home. New Year's Eve is when you go out.

Alain Ducasse

My grandmother did all the cooking at Christmas. We ate fattened chicken. We would feed it even more so it would be big and fat.

Alain Ducasse

I don't know of too many double Christmas albums, so it is something that's new, and hopefully will be fun, and there's plenty of stuff out there to cut.

Garth Brooks

As a very young man growing up in Texas, usually I got a shotgun or cowboy boots for Christmas.

Robert Wilson

When I grew up, we always had our chickens, and we ate

our eggs, and we ate our chickens. The family always had a pig, and we would kill it at Christmas and eat it for three or four months afterwards.

Isabella Rossellini

Dickens was a part of how the whole celebration of Christmas as we know it today emerged during the 19th century.

Claire Tomalin

To understand this Christmas record, you have to understand our ministry.

John Tesh

Some bands today have the experience of really working together and honing their craft. And other bands are very much like, 'I just got a guitar for Christmas, let's start a band.' And you can hear the difference.

Robbie Robertson

Halloween starts earlier and earlier, just like Christmas.

Robert Englund

My grandson sees me as Lois on TV every Christmas, and that scores me points.

Margot Kidder

The first music I was ever exposed to was Irish folk music, like the Clancy Brothers. My father plays that and Christmas songs.

Matt Dillon

The most classic French dessert around the holidays is the Christmas log, with butter cream. Two flavors. Chocolate and coconut. My first job in the kitchen when I was a boy was to make these Christmas logs.

Alain Ducasse

My mother would give my brothers and me a pile of catalogues and let us pick what we wanted for Christmas.

Kary Mullis

My Christmas wish would be to have an entire week off. To spend it with my family and just curl up and watch

Christmas movies when it's snowing outside.

David Hasselhoff

I'm learning Spanish - I got Rosetta Stone for Christmas.

Karlie Kloss

My father used to always give me a basketball, a skate board, and a bike every Christmas. That's all I wanted every year.

Amar'e Stoudemire

My parents got me a $25 Kent steel-string acoustic guitar when I was around 12. The following Christmas, my parents bought me a Conora electric guitar. It looked almost like a Gretsch. It cost $59, and my mom still has it.

Alex Lifeson

My mother died of metastatic colorectal cancer shortly before three P.M. on Christmas Day of 2008. I don't know the exact time of her death, because none of us thought to look at a clock for a while after she stopped breathing.

Meghan O'Rourke

I loved 'White Christmas' for the music aspect. I was into musical theater.

Lana Parrilla

A title means marketing. It means that company's coming soon, and you'd better get out the Christmas lights so they don't miss your house.

Caroline Leavitt

Why not collect and clean chicken wishbones in the run-up to Christmas, spray them silver and use each to pinch together a white hem-stitch napkin?

Pippa Middleton

My wife's brother has a little house on a small island in the Baltic Sea, and we go there at Christmas. The 30-minute crossing from the mainland to this island is the most terrifying cruise you'll ever take. They give you a barf bag when you walk on board.

Nick Frost

I read everything. I'll read a John Grisham novel, I'll sit and read a whole book of poems by Maya Angelou, or I'll just read some Mary Oliver - this is a book that was given to me for Christmas. No particular genre. And I read in French, and I read in German, and I read in English. I love to see how other people use language.

Jessye Norman

I'm going to take the kids away over Christmas but I don't, I've written 14 musicals now, I don't want to rush into doing something just for the sake of doing it. I want to do it when I find a story.

Andrew Lloyd Webber

I used to know Jennifer Love Hewitt. We lived in the same apartment building when I was about... jeez, I guess it was when I was doing 'Christmas Vacation', so I was about 13 or 14.

Johnny Galecki

I picked up the guitar at 12 yrs old - basically, my mother and father bought it for me for Christmas. I played one at my friend's house; when I say played it, I just played around with it at my friend's house. It just struck me as something I really wanted.

Greg Lake

Farmers' markets are one of my favourite sources for Christmas goodies.

Sheherazade Goldsmith

I watched a lot of movies when I was younger and I remember, when I was seven years old, I asked my parents if I could have an agent for Christmas.

Meaghan Rath

I think we need one recognized, respected public figure to make a tough, blunt statement on just what Reagan's record is and what he might do to the country, let alone the Republican Party before Christmas.

Robert Teeter

There's a little Christmas in all of us, I guess. Even in me.

Leon Redbone

Besides the two Christmas things, we've got a about a

dozen new tracks we're working on.

Chris Frantz

I made a Christmas album a couple of years ago and just put it out on my Web site. It kind of smacked of this flavor. All of the reviews said it was Western swing even when it was Christmas standards.

Suzy Bogguss

When 'I'm Sorry' came out and became such a huge hit, that made 'Rockin' Around The Christmas Tree' start selling. Then that became a huge, huge hit.

Brenda Lee

Our last jam session was this past Christmas. Dad played his harmonica, mom sang in English and Italian, and I played guitar. I'm so happy that we could share that musical experience for one last time.

Tony Visconti

Our whole family assembles in Chicago at Christmas and usually in Aspen in the summer.

James Cronin

I don't go back home to Sardinia as much as I would like, just for Christmas and family events.

Caterina Murino

I've also just finished filming the role of Robert Brown in 'Just William,' which is due to transmit on BBC One at Christmas.

Harry Melling

So when I was 13, I basically left home and never returned and lived at home again. I would come home for a week at Christmas and two weeks in the summer only.

Peter Jurasik

Nothing is as peaceful as when Christmas is over, when one has been forgiven for everything and can be normal again.

Tove Jansson

Christmas always rustled. It rustled every time, mysteriously, with silver and gold paper, tissue paper and a rich abundance of shiny paper, decorating and hiding everything and giving a feeling of reckless extravagance.

Tove Jansson

Mummy weighed sweets and nuts so that everyone would get exactly the same amount. During the year, everything is measured roughly, but at Christmas, it has to be absolutely fair. That's why it's such a strenuous time.

Tove Jansson

On the morning, Daddy and I get up at six o'clock because Christmas trees must be bought in the dark. We walk to the other end of town, as the big harbour is just the right setting for buying a Christmas tree. We spend hours choosing, looking at every branch suspiciously. It's always cold.

Tove Jansson

I went on iTunes and looked at versions of Christmas songs. Everyone has done them!

Vince Clarke

I love writing Christmas stories, especially of the historical variety.

Linda Lael Miller

I've also committed my time and resources to many local organizations like Christmas in April, Catholic Community Services, and Hudson County Meals on Wheels.

Vincent Frank

I remember as a child, my mother loved Dean Martin. Every Christmas, about the only Christmas album that we were able to listen to was the Dean Martin Christmas album.

Michael Spradlin

Get FREE Kindle Books Every Week, Delivered by Email!

Click Here or go to quoteoctopus.com to get your free books!